SCRI

Novena
in a time of anxiety

by
Linda Salvatore Boccia, FSP and
Dorothy Anne Perry, FSP

ST PAULS

Original English edition title: *Novena in a Time of Anxiety*
by Linda Salvatore Boccia, FSP and Dorothy Anne Perry, FSP

Copyright © 2001, Daughters of St Paul

The Scripture quotations contained herein are from the *New Revised Standard Version Bible, Catholic Edition*, copyright © 1993 and 1989 by the Division of Christian Education of the National Council of the Churches of Christ in the USA. Used by permission. All rights reserved.

ST PAULS Publishing
187 Battersea Bridge Road, London SW11 3AS, UK
www.stpauls.ie

First published in UK 2002, reprinted 2004, 2007

ISBN 085439 645 4

Set by TuKan DTP, Fareham, Hampshire, UK
Printed by AGAM, Cuneo, Italy

ST PAULS is an activity of the priests and brothers
of the Society of St Paul who proclaim the Gospel
through the media of social communication

What is a Novena?

Most families have traditions – cherished customs and practices handed on from one generation to another. A novena is like that – a Catholic "family tradition," a type of prayer that is one of the ways our family of faith has prayed for centuries.

The Catholic tradition of praying novenas comes from the earliest days of the Church. After the ascension of Jesus, the Acts of the Apostles tells us that the Apostles and Mary gathered together and "joined in constant prayer" (Acts 1:14). And on the day of Pentecost, the Spirit of the Lord came to them. Based on this, Christians have always prayed for various needs, trusting that God both hears and answers prayer. Over time, the custom of praying for nine consecutive days for a particular need came to be called praying "a novena," since *novena* means *nine*.

There are many different kinds of novenas, but their purpose is the same: we call to mind our needs and we ask God's help and protection while remembering how much God loves us. And as we pray, we also ask for a greater understanding and acceptance of God's mysterious workings in our life and the lives of those we love.

"But," we might wonder, "doesn't God know our needs before we even ask; isn't praying once for something enough?" Although we believe in God's love for us, sometimes we need to remind ourselves of this. Although we know we are held in God's hands and that God will not let go, sometimes we need reassurance. In times of darkness, we need something to hold on to; in times of joy, we want to keep rejoicing! What may appear to be mere repetition in a novena is really a continual act of faith and hope in our loving God.

Like the Rosary, the Stations of the Cross, the Liturgy of the Hours, or meal prayers, novenas are one small part of our Catholic faith. The greatest prayer of all is the Eucharistic Celebration. The Eucharist is central to Catholic living; from this great source flows the answer to all our human longings. Through praying with Scripture in this novena, may we draw near our Eucharistic God with confidence, "to receive mercy and find grace to help us in time of need" (Heb 4:16).

Novena in times of anxiety

If we read the daily paper or watch the nightly news, we find more than enough reasons to feel anxious. The twists and turns of strained international relations, the ups and downs of the economy, the ins and outs of the health care industry, and countless other uncertainties, can all contribute to our feeling anxious. When we combine these larger reasons for anxiety with our personal worries over the past, present, or future, things could appear rather grim. Yet we have every reason to hope in our God whose loving care is constant. Even when we feel life is a dangerous balancing act over turbulent waters of anxiety, God is our sure footing. Our reasons for anxiety may not disappear, but we can hold on confidently to Jesus' assurance that we need not worry about our lives (cf. Lk 12:11).

To be done on a daily basis

For nine consecutive days, set apart time for quiet reflection on the true meaning of your life. The title given to each day is the theme for that day. Try to centre your meditation on the biblical thoughts suggested for the day in light of this theme, and bear in mind your own needs and desires.

Remind yourself that you are in God's presence. Ask God to bless you and all those you love as you hold in your heart the persons and intentions that you especially desire to pray for. Confidently express these intentions to God.

Pray the *opening prayer*, and then begin to meditate on the day's scripture passage. Allow a slow, peaceful repetition of the Word of God to nourish whatever within you may be barren and dry, anxious and afraid. Try to open your heart to hear the Lord speaking to you about your situation. Pay attention to any unexpected thoughts or feelings that arise during your prayer... is God extending any invitations to you regarding your intentions?

As you come to the end of your prayer time, spend some moments silently recalling the day's theme. End your prayer time by praying an *Our Father*, *Hail Mary*, *Glory Be*, and the *closing prayer*.

Opening prayer
(for each day)

Ever living God, you care for everything you have made. In moments of fear, give us courage; when we are overwhelmed by anxiety, give us renewed faith in your loving providence. We ask this through Jesus, your Son. Amen.

Closing prayer
(also shown at the end of each day)

Father, we know that your love never fails. Whatever the troubles of our hearts, you guide and sustain us. May the beauty of your creation – the lilies of the field and ravens of the air (cf. Lk 12:24, 27) – be a constant reminder to us that nothing you have made is ever forgotten. Grant this through Jesus Christ your Son, who is Lord forever and ever. Amen.

Day 1

God is with us

Opening prayer (page 10)

For meditation

How long, O LORD?
Will you forget me forever?
How long will you hide your face from me?
How long must I bear pain in my soul,
and have sorrow in my heart all day long?
Consider and answer me, O LORD my God!
Give light to my eyes...
I trusted in your steadfast love;
my heart shall rejoice in your salvation.
I will sing to the LORD,
because he has dealt bountifully with me.

Psalm 13:1–2, 3, 5–6

"And remember, I am always with you, to the end of the age."

Matthew 28:20

To recall throughout the day

When I thought, "My foot is slipping," your steadfast love, O LORD, held me up. When the cares of my heart are many, your consolations cheer my soul.

Psalm 94:18–19

Closing prayer

Father, we know that your love never fails. Whatever the troubles of our hearts, you guide and sustain us. May the beauty of your creation – the lilies of the field and ravens of the air (cf. Lk 12:24, 27) – be a constant reminder to us that nothing you have made is ever forgotten. Grant this through Jesus Christ your Son, who is Lord forever and ever. Amen.

Day 2

God is our refuge

Opening prayer (page 10)

For meditation

The LORD is my rock, my fortress, and
    my deliverer,
my God, my rock in whom I take refuge,
my shield, and the horn of my salvation,
    my stronghold.
I call upon the LORD.

Psalm 18:2–3

Thus says the LORD, he who created you,
    O Jacob,
he who formed you, O Israel.
do not fear, for I have redeemed you;
I have called you by name, you are mine.
When you pass through the waters, I will
    be with you;
and through the rivers, they shall not
    overwhelm you;
when you walk through fire you shall not
    be burned,

and the flame shall not consume you.
For I am the LORD your God,
the Holy One of Israel, your Saviour.
Because you are precious in my sight,
and honoured, and I love you.
Do not fear, for I am with you.

Isaiah 43:1–2, 4–5

To recall throughout the day

When I thought, "My foot is slipping," your steadfast love, O LORD, held me up. When the cares of my heart are many, your consolations cheer my soul.

Psalm 94 18–19

Closing prayer

Father, we know that your love never fails. Whatever the troubles of our hearts, you guide and sustain us. May the beauty of your creation – the lilies of the field and ravens of the air (cf. Lk 12:24, 27) – be a constant reminder to us that nothing you have made is ever forgotten. Grant this through Jesus Christ your Son, who is Lord forever and ever. Amen.

Day 3

God remembers us always

Opening prayer (page 10)

For meditation

Sing for joy, O heavens, and exult, O earth;
break forth, O mountains, into singing!
For the LORD has comforted his people,
and will have compassion on his suffering
   ones.
But Zion said, "The LORD has forsaken me,
my LORD has forgotten me."
Can a woman forget her nursing child,
or show no compassion for the child of her
   womb?
Even these may forget,
yet I will not forget you.
See, I have inscribed you on the palms of
   my hands.

Isaiah 49:13–16

"Peace I leave with you; my peace I give to you. I do not give to you as the world gives. Do not let your hearts be troubled, and do not let them be afraid."

John 14:27

To recall throughout the day

When I thought, "My foot is slipping," your steadfast love, O LORD, held me up. When the cares of my heart are many, your consolations cheer my soul.

Psalm 94:18–19

Closing prayer

Father, we know that your love never fails. Whatever the troubles of our hearts, you guide and sustain us. May the beauty of your creation – the lilies of the field and ravens of the air (cf. Lk 12:24, 27) – be a constant reminder to us that nothing you have made is ever forgotten. Grant this through Jesus Christ your Son, who is Lord forever and ever. Amen.

Day 4

God knows our needs

Opening prayer (page 10)

For meditation

The LORD is my light and my salvation;
whom shall I fear?
The LORD is the stronghold of my life;
of whom shall I be afraid?
Hear, O LORD, when I cry aloud,
be gracious to me and answer me!
Do not hide your face from me.
Do not turn your servant away in anger,
you who have been my help.
Do not cast me off, do not forsake me.
O God of my salvation!

If my father and mother forsake me,
the LORD will take me up.

Psalm 27:1, 7, 9–10

"Very truly, I tell you, if you ask anything of the Father in my name, he will give it to you. Ask and you will receive."

John 15:23

To recall throughout the day

When I thought, "My foot is slipping," your steadfast love, O LORD, held me up. When the cares of my heart are many, your consolations cheer my soul.

Psalm 94:18–19

Closing prayer

Father, we know that your love never fails. Whatever the troubles of our hearts, you guide and sustain us. May the beauty of your creation – the lilies of the field and ravens of the air (cf. Lk 12:24, 27) – be a constant reminder to us that nothing you have made is ever forgotten. Grant this through Jesus Christ your Son, who is Lord forever and ever. Amen.

Day 5

God cares for us

Opening prayer (page 10)

For meditation

"Ask, and it will be given you; search, and you will find, knock, and the door will be opened for you. For everyone who asks receives, and everyone who searches finds, and for everyone who knocks, the door will be opened. Is there anyone among you who, if your child asks for bread, will give a stone? Or if the child asks for a fish, will give a snake? If you then, who are evil, know how to give good gifts to your children, how much more will your Father in heaven give good things to those who ask him!"

Matthew 7:7–11

To recall throughout the day

When I thought, "My foot is slipping," your steadfast love, O LORD, held me up. When the cares of my heart are many, your consolations cheer my soul.

Psalm 94:18–19

Closing prayer

Father, we know that your love never fails. Whatever the troubles of our hearts, you guide and sustain us. May the beauty of your creation – the lilies of the field and ravens of the air (cf. Lk 12:24, 27) – be a constant reminder to us that nothing you have made is ever forgotten. Grant this through Jesus Christ your Son, who is Lord forever and ever. Amen.

Day 6

Give God your worries

Opening prayer (page 10)

For meditation

"Therefore I tell you, do not worry about your life, what you will eat, or about your body, what you will wear. For life is more than food, and the body more than clothing... Consider the lilies, how they grow they neither toil nor spin; yet I tell you, even Solomon in all his glory was not clothed like one of these. But if God so clothes the grass of the field, which is alive today and tomorrow is thrown into the oven, how much more will he clothe you – you of little faith! Do not be afraid, little flock, for it is your Father's good pleasure to give you the kingdom."

Luke 12:22–23, 27–28, 32

To recall throughout the day

When I thought, "My foot is slipping," your steadfast love, O LORD, held me up. When the cares of my heart are many, your consolations cheer my soul.

Psalm 94:18–19

Closing prayer

Father, we know that your love never fails. Whatever the troubles of our hearts, you guide and sustain us. May the beauty of your creation – the lilies of the field and ravens of the air (cf. Lk 12:24, 27) – be a constant reminder to us that nothing you have made is ever forgotten. Grant this through Jesus Christ your Son, who is Lord forever and ever. Amen.

Day 7

God is our joy

Opening prayer (page 10)

For meditation

Protect me, O God, for in you I take refuge.
I say to the LORD, "You are my Lord;
I have no good apart from you."
I bless the LORD who gives me counsel;
in the night also my heart instructs me.
I keep the LORD always before me;
because he is at my right hand,
I shall not be moved.
You show me the path of life,
in your presence there is fullness of joy;
in your right hand are pleasures forevermore.

Psalm 16:1–2, 7–8, 11

To recall throughout the day

When I thought, "My foot is slipping," your steadfast love, O LORD, held me up. When the cares of my heart are many, your consolations cheer my soul.

Psalm 94:18–19

Closing prayer

Father, we know that your love never fails. Whatever the troubles of our hearts, you guide and sustain us. May the beauty of your creation – the lilies of the field and ravens of the air (cf. Lk 12:24, 27) – be a constant reminder to us that nothing you have made is ever forgotten. Grant this through Jesus Christ your Son, who is Lord forever and ever. Amen.

Day 8

God heals us

Opening prayer (page 10)

For meditation

I am going to bring it [Jerusalem] recovery and healing; I will heal them and reveal to them abundance of prosperity and security. I will restore the fortunes of Judah and the fortunes of Israel, and rebuild them as they were at first. I will cleanse them from all the guilt of their sin against me, and I will forgive all the guilt of their sin and rebellion against me. And this city shall be to me a name of joy, a praise and a glory before all the nations of the earth who shall hear of all the good that I do for them; they shall fear and tremble because of all the good and all the prosperity I provide for it.

Jeremiah 33:6–9

To recall throughout the day

When I thought, "My foot is slipping," your steadfast love, O LORD, held me up. When the cares of my heart are many, your consolations cheer my soul.

Psalm 94:18–19

Closing prayer

Father, we know that your love never fails. Whatever the troubles of our hearts, you guide and sustain us. May the beauty of your creation – the lilies of the field and ravens of the air (cf. Lk 12:24, 27) – be a constant reminder to us that nothing you have made is ever forgotten. Grant this through Jesus Christ your Son, who is Lord forever and ever. Amen.

Day 9

God leads us

Opening prayer (page 10)

For meditation

To you, O LORD, I lift up my soul,
my God, in you I trust;
do not let me be put to shame;
do not let my enemies exult over me.
Make me know your ways, O LORD;
teach me your paths.
Lead me in your truth, and teach me,
for you are the God of my salvation;
for you I wait all day long.
Turn to me and be gracious to me,
for I am lonely and afflicted.
Relieve the troubles of my heart,
and bring me out of my distress.
Consider my affliction and my trouble,
and forgive all my sins.

Psalm 25:1–2, 4–5, 18

To recall throughout the day

When I thought, "My foot is slipping," your steadfast love, O LORD, held me up. When the cares of my heart are many, your consolations cheer my soul.

Psalm 94:18–19

Closing prayer

Father, we know that your love never fails. Whatever the troubles of our hearts, you guide and sustain us. May the beauty of your creation – the lilies of the field and ravens of the air (cf. Luke 12:24, 27) – be a constant reminder to us that nothing you have made is ever forgotten. Grant this through Jesus Christ your Son, who is Lord forever and ever. Amen.

Titles in the same series of *Scripture Novenas*

Novena in a Time of Grief

Novena in a Time of Depression

Novena in a Time of Difficulty